NAMES FOR CATS

BY

Michael Mosley

This book is dedicated to anyone who wants to name their cat a unique name.

Simply look through the list of names (A-Z) and you may find a name for your cute furry friend.

Good luck, and God bless.

A: ABE ABEL ARNIE ANGEL ABBIE ASPEN ARTLE
ANDAL ARBIE APPLE ASPER ALLIE ALLEY ART

B: BEN BENNIE BALLY BENSON BIPPY BINKY BOO

BORIS BRACE BRACKET BLAZE BLACKIE BEANS

C: CAMPY CRUISE CRUISER CECIL CABBAGE CALE CINDY CANTY CASEY CALLEE CANTRO CARIE

D: DIXIE DANDELION DANA DANUBE DANIEL DIX
DESSIE DARLING DEZZIE DIESEL DOBBS

E: EMA EFFIE ENUS EPOCH ERBY ERIN ERTLE
EADIE EVAL EARNIE ENDAL ELVIS EASY

F: FILBERT FINNY FLOSSIE FARIS FLIPPER FIGGY
FLORENCE FENTON FALE FAIL FURRY

G: GENO GENA GANDER GILLIE GUSTAVE GOLDIE GILBERT GROVER GONDO

H: HILLIE HARRY HARTLEY HANNIBEL HORTENSE
HALLIE HUCK HINTON HANLEE HARRIET
HANNAH

I: INA ITSY IFFY INEZ IRMA INTRO INSLEY IFFIE IRKIE ISABEL IRVIN IRVANNA IMMA

J: JILL JILLIE JUNIPER JESUS JESTER JASPER JUMPER JULES JILES

K: KILLER KWON KASPER KALEY KING KALE

KWEENIE

L: LYLE LILLY LUDWIG LEENA LESTER LOIS
LOTTIE LIKEY LOLLY LANDERS LUFTWIG
LORIS

M: MILLIE MELVIN MELVINNA MYLA MILDRED
MEANA MOLLY MINLOW MINNOW MILEY
MAURICE MORRIS MORT MENCHEW

N: NILES NORRIS NELLIE NOLBERT NEICIE

NILLY NELLY NICE NEPTUNE NEDDY NEDDIE

NOLIN NINA NOREEN

O: ORO OTIS ONION O-RING ORDER ONNIT

OBLONG OLIVE OLIVIA ONYA OSCAR

OLIVER

P: PHILO PHENA PHRINA PHARIS PHUZZIE
PHREENA PHESTER POPPIE POPPY PARIS

Q: QUEENIE QUEEN QUESTER QUITTER Q-TIP QUINTON

R: RILEY RIDER RINNEY RENE ROBIN
RENLOW

S: STAR STOMPER STILES SHERONA

T: TILLIE TEX TESSIE TINA TUSSEL TWIXXIE

U: UNA UMA URBAN URBANNA

V: VINNIE VANCE VINCENT VALIANT VESTER VANDAL VAMPER

W: WILLIE WESTER WILLIS WHITEY WILDER

WORLEY WHITE-WASH WOOLEY

X: XENA XYLER XANTHEM XAXBY

Y: YANIE YELLOW YULE YETTA YANNIE YALE YELLER

Z: ZENA ZANNA ZOEY ZOREEN ZORINE ZORINA